Canada's System of Government

Weigl Educational Publishers Limited

Published by Weigl Educational Publishers Limited
6325 – 10 Street SE
Calgary, Alberta, Canada
T2H 2Z9

Web site: www.weigl.com

All of the Internet URLs given in the book were valid at the time of publication.
However, due to the dynamic nature of the Internet, some addresses may have
changed, or sites may have ceased to exist since publication. While the author and
publisher regret any inconvenience this may cause readers, no responsibility for any
such changes can be accepted by either the author or the publisher.

Library and Archives Canada Cataloguing in Publication
        Canada's system of government / Don Wells, editor.
(Canadian government)
Includes index.
ISBN 1-55388-071-4 (bound) ISBN 1-55388-126-5 (pbk)
        1. Regionalism--Canada--Textbooks. 2. Canada--Textbooks.
I. Wells, Don, 1953- II. Series: Canadian government (Calgary, Alta.)
FC57.C3558 2004   971   C2004-903630-0

Printed in the United States of America
1 2 3 4 5 6 7 8 9 0   09 08 07 06 05 04

We acknowledge the
financial support of the
Government of Canada
through the Book
Publishing Industry
Development Program
(BPIDP) for our
publishing activities.

Editor
Don Wells

Copy Editor
Tina Schwartzenberger

Photo Researcher
Ellen Byran

Designer
Warren Clark

Layout
Terry Paulhus

On the Cover
Fireworks on Parliament
Hill are a popular part of
Canada Day celebrations
in Ottawa.

Contents

Canada's Government

The Centre Block of the Parliament buildings contains the Peace Tower. This tower commemorates Canada's commitment to peace.

Can you imagine how different things would be if there was no government? There would be no laws governing how fast we drive, how our hospitals are managed, or even what we learn in school. Almost every aspect of our lives is touched by government decisions. The process of reaching these decisions—politics—can often be long and complicated.

Canada's system of government and politics has been developed on the basis of principles and systems inherited mainly from Western European political systems. In some cases, these principles have been adapted to suit unique Canadian circumstances.

The structure of government in Canada is based on the principle of representative democracy and other principles inherited from the political practices of Western Europe. To more efficiently make decisions for Canadians, our government has divided decision-making authority among several levels of government, with each responsible for looking after different needs.

The federal government manages issues of concern to all Canadians. Provincial and territorial governments administer the needs of the provinces

and territories. Municipal governments make laws for cities and towns. Some Aboriginal Peoples also have their own governments, called band councils. Band councils administer the concerns of communities living on reserves.

Canadian government relies on responsible **citizenship**. Responsible citizenship means understanding the roles, **rights**, and responsibilities of individuals in a democratic society and participating in the democratic process by making rational and informed decisions. Citizens require a wide background of knowledge and skills to keep pace with changes in our society.

IN-DEPTH

Other Systems of Government

Some countries are ruled by governments known as dictatorships. In dictatorships such as the one that ruled Germany during the 1930s and 1940s, citizens do not play a role in government processes. The leader or leaders make laws, decide on policies, and plan the goals of the nation. If elections are held, citizens often only vote for one candidate or select one of a few candidates from the same **political party**. There may be no political parties with differing points of view. Citizens in dictatorships have less influence than citizens in democracies.

A government in which one person has all the **power** is called an autocracy, such as Saudi Arabia, which is ruled by a king. Outside of the Middle East, there are few examples of this type of government.

A country ruled by a small group of leaders is an oligarchy. This type of government ruled the Canadian colonies before the introduction of responsible government. A country with only one political party has a totalitarian government. The

■ *China has followed a communist model of one-party rule since 1949.*

Soviet Union was thought to be a totalitarian government.

The main features of these types of government is the inability of individual citizens to have a real impact on the decision-making process. Citizens in countries ruled by these governments have less power than citizens in most democracies. These states place greater value on state need than on individual needs.

FURTHER UNDERSTANDING
Band

The term band is used to describe a group of Aboriginal People who have reserve lands or money held by the Canadian government. Bands include groups that were traditionally organized as tribes—usually a group of people related by blood or marriage—or chiefdoms—the people or territory over which a chief rules. Canada has more than 600 bands. They act as small Aboriginal municipalities. Bands are managed by elected band councils. Bands sometimes include people with different cultures and languages.

Politics

> It would be inefficient, and clearly dangerous, to live in a society where everyone did exactly as they pleased.

Politics is a process of making decisions that affect relationships between people. Political decisions are rarely straightforward because they seldom fully satisfy the goals or needs of everyone involved. People have different opinions about the issues that affect their lives. The process of deciding which needs or whose interests will prevail is a political one.

Most people think of politics in its institutional form. This kind of politics involves governments, elections, and the business of managing the concerns of large population groups. Decisions about how much tax people should pay, how fast people can drive, and whether citizens must wear helmets when riding motorcycles are all types of decisions made by an institutionalized political process. Systems of government and elections to choose government leaders are institutions set up to manage the business of politics.

Decision making can be difficult at the national, provincial, territorial, and municipal levels. Decision making becomes more difficult as the number of people affected by decisions increases. Before making decisions, many governments, consult with individuals, unions, other levels of government, lobbyists, and special **interest groups**. As the number of demands increase, the likelihood of a decision that satisfies everyone decreases. This is why few political decisions make the entire population happy and why the political process is sometimes viewed unfavourably.

It would be inefficient, and clearly dangerous, to live in a society where everyone did exactly as they pleased. It makes sense for people to join together to ensure there are rules that govern their society and make it possible for people to interact with some assurance of safety and predictability.

Romania's communist government suppressed anti-government demonstrations before it collapsed in 1989.

Voicing an Opinion on an Issue

In the Canadian system of democracy, citizens have the ability to affect and make important decisions. Two high school students in Red Deer, Alberta, learned that lesson when they voiced their opinions about a proposed petrochemical plant.

Grade 11 students Rene McMullen and Kathy Murdoch decided to get involved in a serious issue. Through the local media, they heard about plans for a new petrochemical plant just outside Red Deer. The two decided to explore the issue for a class project.

After some research, the students learned that Alberta Gas Ethylene Co. Ltd. (AGE) was seeking permission to build a $370 million plant to make ethylene, a colourless, flammable gas with an unpleasant odour. Ethylene is used to make plastic, baler twine, and film.

The students gathered this information from local sources, but they could not tell how the plant's daily operations would affect the environment.

"We didn't know anything about it and started from scratch," Murdoch later told a writer with *Environment Views*. "That was the beginning of our frustration. We found it difficult to get information, and when we got some, it was often contradictory."

For example, some sources claimed the initial plant would use 1.7 cubic metres of water per second, and a second similar plant would require 2.27 cubic metres of water per second. Later, those numbers dropped to 0.2 cubic metres and 0.25 cubic metres per second. The students wanted precise statistics.

Murdoch and McMullen wrote a letter titled "Questions that Deserve Answers" and mailed it to a local newspaper. The letter was printed, and AGE responded. The company sent several representatives to Murdoch and McMullen's school to discuss the students' concerns, but the visit was not enough for Murdoch and McMullen. The pair felt their questions had not been thoroughly answered.

Next, the students decided to attend a **public hearing** on the proposed plant. They decided the use of Alberta's non-renewable resources and the plant's effect on the environment were concerns that needed to be addressed.

Murdoch and McMullen prepared a presentation and distributed it to the Alberta Energy and Utilities Board, which held the meeting.

Speaking for six students, McMullen told the conservation board

■ *In spite of dangers to the environment, chemical plants are often important to a community's economy.*

that the plant's construction should not proceed because the public had not received enough information.

McMullen said the project's effect on the environment should be studied before construction. She also suggested that AGE use the steam and vapor created by the plant for energy or for heating greenhouses.

After the students' presentation, the board called AGE's environment panel back to answer more questions. The board said a number of questions raised by the students had not been adequately answered and the public needed more specific information.

In the end, the plans for the plant were approved without all the requested changes, and AGE started construction. Still, the students felt they had achieved several things:

- AGE officials clarified several contradictory facts.
- The public received more details on a project that would affect Alberta's environment and economy.
- AGE's vice-president publicly supported the use of water vapor to heat greenhouses.
- The students' efforts acted as a model for other youths.

Democracy

In ancient Greece, citizens ruled the city of Athens. All male residents met in public places to discuss issues and reach decisions. Women and slaves were not classified as citizens. The ancient Greeks named this form of government "democracy," which meant "ruled by the people, for the people." Democracy is a way for people to make decisions based upon what is best for the largest number of people—the majority.

There are two forms of democracy: direct and representative. Direct democracy means that every person votes on every issue. Direct democracy occurs in small towns and city neighbourhoods in which people meet to debate issues and decide on a course of action. Many unions are also controlled by direct democracy. Members are encouraged to express their viewpoints and vote on issues.

■ *Greek cities were formed around an acropolis on top of a hill. The acropolis was the centre of public life.*

Direct democracy can also occur on a large scale when governments hold referendums and plebiscites. Canada's referendum on national unity in 1992 was an example of direct democracy at work. This referendum asked voters to vote for or against the Charlottetown Accord. This Accord, which was rejected by voters, would have made fundamental changes to Canada's Constitution.

In a representative democracy, a group of people elect another person to represent their views. Representative democracy has evolved because most countries, including Canada, have too many people for direct democracy to work efficiently. It would take far too long to organize people and listen to everyone's views on every issue. Few Canadians would have time to work or sleep if they also had to participate

in every government decision. Canadians therefore vote for a group of elected representatives who debate issues, establish policies, and make laws to govern everyone. These elected representatives are politicians, people who make the political process their job.

Although the idea of democracy dates back to ancient Greece, it was not always a common part of political systems. At one time, **monarchs** had absolute power, which meant they could make all decisions without consulting anyone. Many people believed that monarchs had direct authority from God to make decisions. Under an absolute monarch, the people had little or no chance to influence the decisions that affected them.

Although Canada has a monarch, the Queen does not have absolute power. Canada's democracy is a constitutional monarchy. The role of the monarch is limited by the Canadian constitution, which ensures that elected representatives make decisions for Canadians.

HISTORY

Iroquois Democracy

Democracy existed in North America long before the first Europeans arrived. The League of the Iroquois was formed in the 1500s to end warring between different tribes. The league was founded by the Mohawk, Oneida, Onondaga, Cayuga, and Seneca people. The Tuscarora joined later. Members of the League were political and military allies, but each member managed its own society.

The League was governed by a council of fifty members called *sachems*. Each nation was represented by a group of eight to fourteen members. Positions on the council were hereditary. When a sachem died, the senior woman in his clan chose his successor from the rest of the men in the family. The new sachem took

Iroquois Democracy

the name of the person he replaced, so the names of the council members did not change.

Council members met each fall in the Onondaga nation. The Onondaga were located in the middle of the territory, and the Onondaga chief had a special place of honour in the League. Issues were presented, discussed, and decided on before addressing the next issue. The council tried to reach decisions that all members could agree upon. If no agreement could be reached, then each nation was free to act in its own manner.

In addition to the League, every nation had chiefs who were elected to rule for life. Family members selected their chiefs. These chiefs formed a council that governed each nation. Chiefs were chosen for their abilities and stature in the community. They were considered servants of the people, rather than masters. If the people did not agree with the actions of a chief, he could be removed from office.

Representative Government

Initially, only men of wealth and property were allowed to vote.

Democracy by itself does not ensure a truly representative government. At various times in Canada's history, many people were excluded from voting or running for political office. Initially, only men of wealth and property were allowed to vote, and Canada's government represented only the interests of these few voters. Over time, other groups were allowed to vote. After years of struggle, Aboriginal Peoples, women, and all men, regardless of their wealth and position, were allowed to vote. The voting age was also lowered from 21 to 18.

Today, every person is entitled to vote, provided that he or she is at least 18 years of age, is a Canadian citizen, and has been living in Canada for at least 1 year immediately preceding the election. There are some exceptions, however, such as judges, who are appointed by the federal government. Others who cannot vote include the chief electoral officer, who is responsible for Canada's federal elections and referendums, returning officers, who are responsible for elections in specific districts, and people who have been found guilty of corrupt practices in other elections. This means some people are not represented in the government because they do not have the right to vote.

When citizens elect an individual to represent their interests at various levels of government, they do so with the understanding that their elected representative will act in the citizens' best interests. The elected person is then responsible to the people who elected him or her to office. If citizens are unhappy with the job their representative does, they can choose to elect someone else in the next election. The reelection of a public official amounts to a stamp of approval by the people the official represents and keeps representatives responsible to those who elected them.

Elections must be called within 5 years of the last election.

PROFILE

Tommy Douglas

Thomas (Tommy) Douglas did not plan a career in politics until he saw the Depression's horrific effect on southern Saskatchewan. The sight of poor, destitute farmers and relief trains handing out food and clothing moved Douglas to enter politics and crusade for reform. His efforts paved the way for medicare and the Canada Pension Plan.

Tommy Douglas was born in Scotland in 1904 and moved to Manitoba in 1919 with his religious, working-class family. He worked briefly as a printer, developed a keen interest in church work, and became a Baptist minister. Douglas viewed Christianity as a social religion. Christians should not only guide people to heaven, he thought, but work to improve life on Earth as well.

The young minister set out to act on his beliefs. In the early 1930s, he began helping Depression-battered people in Weyburn, Saskatchewan. Southern Saskatchewan had been hit hard by the tough economy and drought, and Douglas felt he could not do enough as a minister. He turned to politics.

In the 1935 federal election, Douglas ran as a candidate in a riding near Weyburn. He was

one of the first Co-operative Commonwealth Federation (CCF) members elected to the House of Commons.

In Ottawa, Douglas was quickly recognized as a skilful debater. He promoted his party's ideas about reducing unemployment and rural poverty. He also lashed out at capitalism and scorned the federal government for sinking money into World War II while Canadians struggled to find work at home.

Yet Douglas saw little improvement for people in Saskatchewan. Farmers still fought to keep their land, and many seemed locked in a constant battle with mortgage companies. Welfare did not exist, and Douglas felt he could only aid Saskatchewan from a provincial level. If he were closer to the problem, Douglas thought, he would be better able to win support for sweeping reforms.

In 1944, Douglas left the House of Commons

to become the premier of Saskatchewan and form the first socialist government in North America. This government was influenced by socialism, an economic system that uses centralized planning and distribution and is based on cooperation rather than competition. He held this office for 17 years, while his government developed low-cost insurance, free cancer-treatment centres, and improved highways.

Near the end of this period, Douglas unveiled plans for medicare: a government program designed to provide medical care to all Saskatchewan citizens. Doctors and some citizen groups protested, saying the government had no right to control personal medical care, but Douglas persisted. It was a plan that one day would be widely accepted.

Through his efforts to improve Canadian life, Douglas made democratic socialism part of Canadian politics. He left Saskatchewan in 1961 to become the first leader of the federal New Democratic Party (NDP). Douglas led the NDP until 1971, when he stepped down and became the party's energy critic until 1979.

Responsible Government

In Canada, responsible government refers to the system that keeps the **cabinet** responsible to the House of Commons. Prior to responsible government in Canada, decisions were made by oligarchies, which meant that appointed rather than elected leaders had power. In the 1830s, reformers pushed to implement a system of responsible government in which the executive would be responsible to the elected assembly. Joseph Howe brought responsible government to Nova Scotia in 1848. The United Province of Canada and New Brunswick received responsible government by 1849.

Canada's system of responsible government ensures that the cabinet answers to the House of Commons for its actions and decisions, and through the Commons, to the electorate. This chain of responsibility allows small numbers of people to make decisions, but keeps their decisions responsible to the elected assemblies. This means that the government must have the support

When renovations are made to Canada's Parliament buildings, care is taken to preserve the buildings as a symbol of Canadian democracy.

HISTORY

Joseph Howe

In 1835, Joseph Howe, the editor of the *NovaScotian* newspaper, published a letter in his newspaper exposing the dishonesty of several Halifax judges. He was charged with libel—which means to harm someone's reputation in writing—and was swiftly brought to trial. Howe skillfully conducted his own defence. Speaking to a packed courtroom, he described the injustices of the governmental system. Howe held the courtroom spellbound for more than 6 hours. At times, the audience roared with laughter, and the judge was forced to call for order. At other times, people were reduced to tears. The jury declared Howe not guilty. After the verdict, the excited crowd hoisted him on their shoulders and carried him home. Howe's popularity as a champion of the poor helped him become elected to the Assembly in 1836.

Like the Reformers in Upper and Lower Canada, Howe pushed for responsible government. He once declared:

"In England, the people can breathe the breath of life into their government whenever they please. In this country, the government is like an ancient Egyptian mummy, wrapped up in narrow and antique prejudices, dead and inanimate, but yet likely to last forever."

Howe saw responsible government established in Nova Scotia in 1848.

of at least 50 percent of the elected representatives. The cabinet has power to make many decisions, but it is responsible to the other members of **Parliament** (MPs) in the House of Commons for its decisions.

The system of responsibility also extends to government departments. Elected officials who become ministers over government departments are responsible to the elected assembly for the actions of their departments. If a civil servant makes a serious mistake, the minister in charge of that department may be asked to resign.

Each minister is held responsible for the activities and decisions of his or her department, even if the minister is unaware of these decisions or activities. This system of responsibility ensures that elected officials pay close attention to the activities of people who are paid with public money.

As time has passed, the Canadian system of government has become more democratic and more representative of Canadian society. It is up to citizens to make their government responsible by holding their politicians accountable for the actions of the government.

Issues for Inquiry
Public Role vs. Private Beliefs

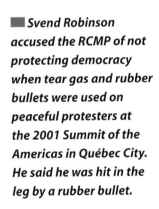

Canadian citizenship is a process in which citizens participate in Canadian life as individuals or members of their communities.

Svend Robinson was a Member of Parliament in the Vancouver area from 1979 to 2004. In April, 1994, Robinson was charged with civil disobedience after participating in a peaceful protest the previous summer against clear-cut logging. The charge was laid against Robinson and the protesters because they were in violation of a court injunction prohibiting the blocking of traffic by protests. Robinson accepted full responsibility for his actions and pled guilty to the charge.

As an ordinary citizen, Robinson's actions, although ruled illegal by the courts, would have been considered no different than those of the other protestors. However, as a member of Parliament, he is expected to uphold the laws of Canada. Following his arrest, some Canadians expressed concern about his actions.

In 2004, Robinson pled guilty to stealing a ring from a jewelry auction and was sentenced to 100 hours of community service. He was reported to be suffering from stress at the time. As a result of this incident, Robinson did not run for reelection in the 2004 federal election.

■ *Svend Robinson accused the RCMP of not protecting democracy when tear gas and rubber bullets were used on peaceful protesters at the 2001 Summit of the Americas in Québec City. He said he was hit in the leg by a rubber bullet.*

DOCUMENT

Robinson's Letter Explaining his 1994 Act of Civil Disobedience

Dear Friends:

I am writing with respect to the recent contempt of court proceeding during which I was sentenced for peaceful civil disobedience. As you are aware, this hearing before the B.C. Supreme Court on July 6, and the sentencing proceedings on July 26, arose from my participation in a peaceful protest on July 5 of last year. This followed the decision of the B.C. Government to allow clear-cut logging in the magnificent old growth forests of Clayoquot Sound. In the months following the July 5 protest, over 800 people were arrested and charged for their involvement in peaceful civil disobedience. Many of them have, like me, been sentenced to terms of imprisonment.

My decision to participate in this peaceful protest stemmed from my deep and long-standing concern for protecting endangered temperate rain forest ecosystems and for respecting the rights of Aboriginal Peoples. On July 4, the day before the first protests, I met with elected and hereditary Chiefs of the Nuu-chah-nulth peoples who make up over 45 percent of the population of Clayoquot Sound, have a land

base of 0.5 percent and an unemployment rate of over 70 percent. They shared with me their sense of anger and deep concern that the provincial government had not consulted with them in a meaningful way before announcing the April 13 decision. They also expressed strong opposition to unsustainable logging practices in the Sound, including clear-cut logging, and noted the devastating impact of current logging practices on their salmon spawning streams.

I firmly believe that the public protests and support from across Canada and around the world have resulted in profound changes in the provincial government's policies on Clayoquot Sound. I will continue to speak out

strongly against clear-cut logging in the pristine, unlogged watersheds and islands of Clayoquot Sound. This is essential to protect the biodiversity of this beautiful area which includes three of the five outstanding unlogged watersheds over 5,000 hectares on Vancouver Island.

My involvement in the July 5 protest was undertaken with full knowledge of the possible legal consequences. I have always been prepared to accept these consequences, including the possibility of a sentence of imprisonment. I recognize and respect the concern that a Member of Parliament is elected to enact laws and not break laws. Nevertheless there are certainly rare occasions on which an elected representative, like any other

The protest at Clayoquot Sound was the largest act of civil disobedience in Canadian history.

citizen of this country, may participate in an act of peaceful civil disobedience in an attempt to highlight profound injustices or unfairness. I made every possible effort to persuade my provincial colleagues to reconsider their decision, especially in light of their failure to meaningfully consult the Aboriginal Peoples directly affected. It is clear to me that had it not been for the actions of the over 800 peaceful protestors, the very significant progress made in Clayoquot Sound to date would never have been achieved.

I have always tried to approach my responsibilities as an elected official with honesty and integrity and I hope that even those among you who disagree fundamentally with my stand at this time will respect, if not support, the reasoning that led to my decision.

Yours in solidarity,
Svend J. Robinson, M.P.
Burnaby-Kingsway

Constitutional Monarchy

Queen Elizabeth usually visits Canada to support certain charities or organizations or to celebrate a historic event.

When Canada became a country in 1867, the British Crown was made a part of its government structure. Canada is a constitutional monarchy. This is a form of government established under a constitutional system that acknowledges a hereditary or elected monarch as head of state. Canadian government is carried out on behalf of the monarchy, and **justice** is administered in the courts in the monarch's name.

The monarch's role in Canada's affairs changed when Canada became a sovereign country. As Canada became an independent country, the Crown's role became less political and more symbolic. If the governor general refused to sign a law passed by Parliament, for example, the refusal would be considered a serious breach of Canadian independence. This change in the Crown's role was complete after the Canada Act was passed in 1982. Canadians now swear allegiance to the Queen of Canada, instead of the Queen of England.

Since Canada's Queen lives in London, England, the governor general represents her in Canada, and the lieutenant governors represent her in each province and territory. The prime minister selects and the monarch appoints the governor general. The governor general has two official residences—Rideau Hall in Ottawa and La Citadelle in Québec City. On taking office, a governor general is usually accorded the title "Right Honourable" for life and "His Excellency" or "Her Excellency" for the period in office.

In 1952, Vincent Massey was the first Canadian to be appointed governor general, ending the tradition of a British governor general. At the same time, the custom of alternating French- and English-speaking governors general began.

Governor General Lord Stanley is well known throughout Canada. As Canada's sixth governor general, Lord Stanley instituted the Stanley Cup for hockey excellence.

IN-DEPTH

Governor General Things To Do

1. Sign **bills** so laws are passed.
2. Summon and dissolve Parliament.
3. Deliver speech from the Throne.
4. Preside over swearing in of prime minister, chief justice of the Supreme Court of Canada, cabinet ministers, and members of the Privy Council.
5. Sign state documents.
6. Act as advisor to the prime minister.
7. Identify replacement prime minister if present one dies, resigns, or if Parliament is stalemated.
8. Receive Queen and other members of the royal family.
9. Receive heads of state and other foreign dignitaries.
10. Make state visits to other countries.
11. Award trophies and prizes for achievements such as the Stanley Cup, the Governor General's Literary Awards, and the Governor General's Academic Awards.
12. Promote national identity through public functions such as the New Year's Levee and the summer Garden Party.
13. Officiate at award presentations, building openings, and the unveiling of plaques and works of art.
14. Visit provinces and territories; meet with lieutenant governors.

Canada's Parliament

The British Monarch
Queen Elizabeth II

Canada's Governor General
Adrienne Clarkson

The Senate

The House of Commons

Rule of Law

The Supreme Court Act requires that three of the nine Supreme Court judges be from Québec.

One of the cornerstones of the Canadian government system is the rule of law. Essentially, this means that everyone is subject to the law. No one, no matter how important or powerful, is above the law. This includes members of the government, the prime minister, cabinet ministers, armed forces personnel, the Queen, and the governor general. None of these people or institutions have any power beyond those granted to them by law.

The reason for this system is simple. If anyone were above the law, then they would be free to do whatever they wanted, no matter how badly they hurt others. The rule of law means that every person and institution must operate within Canada's laws. This helps maintain justice and prevents the abuse of power.

Since they remain independent from outside pressures, the courts are used to prevent any abuse of this rule. This principle of judicial independence goes back more than 300 years to the English Act of Settlement of 1701. This act states that judges, although appointed by the king, and now by the cabinet and prime minister, can be removed from their

positions only if both houses of Parliament asked the Crown to remove them. This freedom from government **censure**, except in the case of misconduct, allows judges to act independently and **impartially**. If judges kept their positions depending only on the **benevolence** of the king or government, they would not be very likely to rule against that king or government in the event of a violation of the rule of law.

Canada's Constitution states that almost all courts will be created by provincial legislatures. The judges of these courts, except courts of **probate** in Nova Scotia and New Brunswick, are appointed by the federal government. The judges of the provincial superior courts and the Supreme Court of Canada can only be removed from their positions if the governor general and both houses of Parliament request it. To date, no judge has been removed in such a manner.

The legal system in all of Canada, except Québec, is based on a system of law known as common law. This system evolved from decisions made by the English royal courts of justice since the Norman Conquest in 1066. Common law is a system that includes statutes, which are written laws, and court decisions. Court decisions form many unwritten legal principles, called precedents, especially in matters of law that deal with private matters between individuals such as property ownership, family obligations, and business deals.

Québec follows a legal system based upon a civil code. This system evolved from Roman law. Today, civil codes are found in countries such as France and in their former colonies. A civil code is a set of written principles that guide judicial decisions on matters of private law. Court decisions do not set legal precedents as they do in common law systems.

Although Québec society has undergone many changes, its civil code remained the same until the 1950s. This is due in part to the province's Catholic and French-speaking society, which believed that the province's laws should be kept separate from the rest of Canada's common law.

In 1955, the Québec legislature established the Civil Code Revision Office to bring the Code up to date and prepare revisions. By 1964, most of the badly outdated portions of the Code had been revised, and a more comprehensive review was instituted. Since 1981, the legislature has enacted reforms to the Code that include laws pertaining to people, property, successions, and trusts.

If the governor general is not available to perform his or her job, the senior associate judge of the Supreme Court becomes Administrator of Canada.

Federal Democracy

■ *There are 308 ridings in Canada. One candidate from each riding is elected into the House of Commons.*

Canada's federal government is similar to other federal democracies that try to accommodate central and regional concerns. Canada's system is primarily based on the British Parliamentary system. This government system has three parts. Both parliaments have an elected lower house and appointed upper house, as well as a queen or head of state. In Canada, the queen is represented by the governor general.

The main difference between the Canadian and British parliamentary system is in the upper house. The upper house is another name for the senate. In Canada, the Senate consists of members appointed for life. In Britain, the House of Lords consists of both hereditary members as well as appointed individuals. The House of Lords has similar powers to the Canadian Senate. It can delay, but not stop legislation from the House of Commons. The House of Commons is also known as the lower house. Members of the House of Commons are elected by the citizens of the country.

Canada's federalism is similar to that of the United States. Both governments

share many of the same concerns, but both governments have chosen different solutions that reflect their different histories and development patterns.

One of the main differences between the Canadian and U.S. federal systems is in how the two countries chose to form their upper houses. When the United States won its independence from Great Britain, it wanted to divorce itself from all reminders of the British Crown. The American upper house, or Senate, is therefore elected, not appointed. By electing the Senate, the Americans distanced their senators from the inherited privileges of the House of Lords and British nobility. In the United States, the lower house is called the House of Representatives. Members of the House of Representatives are elected for a 2-year term. Elections take place during presidential election years and through mid-term elections.

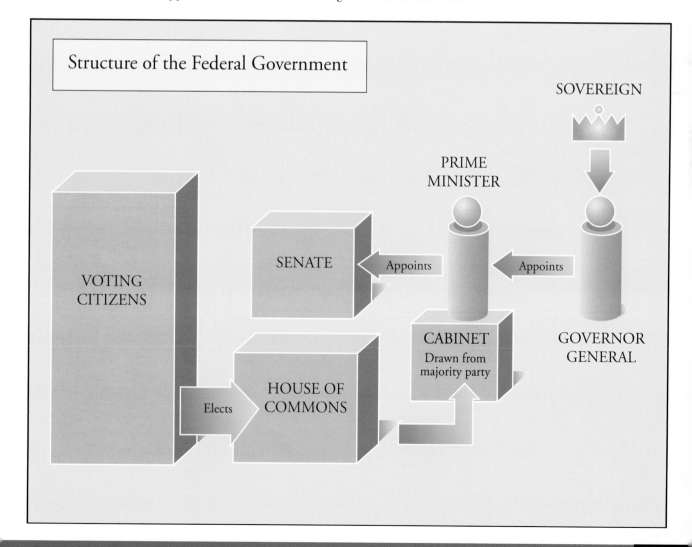

Structure of the Federal Government

SOVEREIGN

PRIME MINISTER

SENATE — Appoints — — Appoints —

VOTING CITIZENS

CABINET
Drawn from majority party

GOVERNOR GENERAL

HOUSE OF COMMONS — Elects

Charting Canada's Government

The Fathers of Confederation thought it was necessary to have a strong central government. They believed that the United States Constitution had created a weak central government and that was the reason for problems such as the American Civil War. However, over time, the United States has strengthened the central government, while Canada has become more decentralized. Today, Canada has one of the most decentralized systems of government in the world. In Canada, power is divided between Canada's provinces and federal government. If there is a dispute about power, the federal government claims **jurisdiction**.

Canadian Federalism **Constitutional Monarchy**	**American Federalism** **Republic**
Parliamentary-Cabinet government	Presidential-Congressional government
Head of state is the Queen, usually represented by the governor general. The head of state serves as a check on the powers of the prime minister and his or her cabinet.	Head of state is the president.
Head of government is the prime minister.	Head of government is the president.
The prime minister and every minister must, by custom, be members of either the House of Commons or the senate.	The president and members of his or her cabinet cannot be members of either the House of Representatives or the senate.
Government bills need to be introduced and defended by a minister or someone speaking on behalf of the minister.	A president and his or her cabinet may not introduce or defend bills in the House. Rather, they must get senators or representatives to do so.
No one is elected for a fixed term. Rather, the government keeps its power as long as it keeps a majority in the House of Commons, with the restriction that an election must be called at least once every 5 years.	The president and House members are elected for a fixed term: the president for 4 years; senators for 6 years; and members of the House of Representatives for 2 years. Power is kept for the full term of office.
If the government loses its majority support in the House of Commons, it must either step aside and allow the opposition to form a government, or call an election to form a new House of Commons. The government and House of Commons cannot be deadlocked for more than a few weeks at a time.	If the president and the majority of Congress belong to different parties (as often happens with fixed-term elections), the president could find his or her bills and policies blocked by the opposition majority. This can result in a stalemate that could last for years.

Division of Powers in Canada

Federal Powers

Taxation (direct and indirect)

Public debt and property

Defence

Post Office

Census and statistics

Beacons, buoys, and lighthouses

Interest rates

Navigation and shipping

Criminal law

The Fisheries (coastal and inland)

Currency and coinage

Broadcasting

Banking, incorporation of banks, and the issue of paper money

Bankruptcy and insolvency

Weights and measures

Air navigation

Patents and copyrights

Penitentiaries

Aboriginal Peoples and the lands reserved for Aboriginal Peoples

Naturalization and aliens

Marriage and divorce laws

Unemployment insurance

Any subject area not specifically controlled by the provinces

Provincial Powers

Civil law

Direct taxation in the province

Hospitals

Education

Natural resources

Provincial prisons

Municipal institutions

Local works and undertakings

Licences for provincial and municipal revenue

Solemnization of marriage

Incorporation of provincial companies

Provincial courts

Property and civil rights in the province

Social security (not unemployment insurance)

Labour legislation (hours, wages, compensation)

Borrowing money on provincial credit

Fines for breaking provincial laws

Management and sale of public lands

Provincial civil service

Note: The territorial governments (Yukon Territory, Northwest Territories, and Nunavut) have more or less the same powers as the provinces. However, territorial governments do not control land and natural resources. Also, their powers are not guaranteed by the Constitution. Territorial government powers are granted by the federal government.

The Federal Government

A ceremonial guard represents the role of Parliament Hill as the centre of Canada's federal government.

When the Fathers of Confederation drafted Canada's Constitution, they had to divide powers between the provinces and the federal government. The Constitution stated that Parliament had the power to make laws for "Peace, Order and Good Government in Canada in relation to all Matters not coming within the classes of subjects by this Act assigned exclusively to the Legislatures of the Provinces." This clause was intended to give the federal government more power than its provincial counterparts.

Since that time, federal and provincial government powers have changed. For example, in 1930, the three prairie provinces received control over their natural resources. In 1982, the provinces received more flexibility when taxing these resources.

Since the Constitution Act was passed in 1982, many Canadians have proposed changes to the division of powers in Canada. Some people, known as centralists, want the federal government to have more power in relation to the provincial governments. They believe the federal government can develop policies that will better enhance Canadian unity. Other people, the decentralists, favour provincial governments with a greater balance of power. These people believe the country is too large and diverse to make a highly centralized government practical.

Throughout Canada's history, most of the federal government's basic powers have remained unchanged. The federal government has the power to defend Canada. This means the government can recruit men and women to serve in the armed forces. It can equip and train these soldiers and purchase military equipment such as tanks, ships, and planes. The government also decides when these troops should be sent to other countries.

The federal government must also provide information about the country and its population. Statistics Canada is a federal government agency that collects statistics such as employment and inflation rates. The federal government also manages Canada's system of money and banking. The federal government decides what kind of coins and paper money Canadians use, as well as whether a new bank can be opened.

The Royal Canadian Mint is a global leader in minting. It is recognized worldwide for its quality and craftsmanship in the production of both circulation and collector coins. It is highly respected as a premier refiner of gold.

IN-DEPTH

Residuary Powers

All federal constitutions, in one way or another, divide power between two levels of government. However, it is not possible for constitution makers to provide a complete list of powers. Something may be forgotten, or new fields of jurisdiction can appear in the future. It is, therefore, necessary for constitution makers to include a clause that determines which of the two levels of government will have those new powers. This is usually called the residuary clause.

In Canada, residuary powers were given to the federal government. The Fathers of Confederation did not want to follow the American Constitution, which gave all residual powers to the individual states. At the time of Confederation, Canada needed a strong federal government that had large enough powers to withstand American pressures and create a strong national economy. The Fathers of Confederation believed that, in the future, the residuary powers would ensure the continued strength of the Dominion government.

Provincial Governments

Canadians do not pay directly for medical services, and there is no dollar limit on insured medical services.

Provincial governments are in charge of such things as education and taxes. This is why a student in New Brunswick, for example, does not have to study exactly the same things as a student in Alberta. A province also has the power to charge a provincial sales tax on all the items you buy.

One of the most important provincial powers is the control of forests and resources such as uranium or oil that are found in the province. This is an important power because these resources can provide provinces with great wealth, rivalling even that of the federal government. Provinces also have the duty to provide health care. Hospitals, doctors, and nurses are all managed by provincial governments.

There are some areas in which the federal and provincial governments share powers. These areas include: agriculture, immigration, certain aspects of natural resources, and pensions. If federal and provincial laws conflict, then federal law supersedes provincial law in all areas except pensions.

Although the powers of each level of government have been written down, there are occasions when it is difficult to tell which level actually has jurisdiction. This can lead to tension between federal and provincial governments. In the 1990s, for example, the provinces and the federal government disagreed about health care reform. The management of health care is a provincial power. However, the federal government actively funds provincial health care systems, and the Canada Health Act, passed unanimously by Parliament in 1984, ensures that Canadians have access to a universal, publicly administered health insurance system. As a result, both the provinces and the federal government feel they have the power to make changes to the health care system. Although disagreements may occur, neither government can alter or dissolve the other's powers without its consent.

Canada's division of powers is similar to other countries that have diverse regions with citizens from a large number of different cultures, language groups, or religions. A federal system gives these groups significant control over how they are governed.

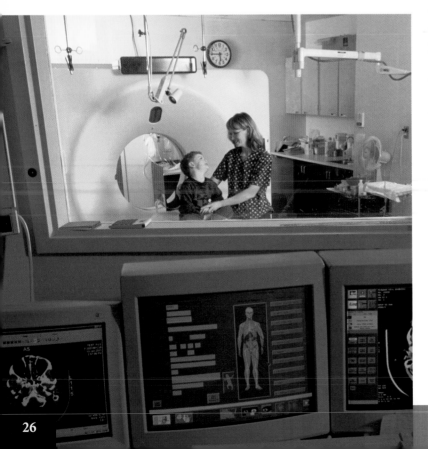

ACTIVE CITIZENSHIP

Challenging Provincial Power

Kim Maier is an Alberta man who disagreed with the province's seat-belt law. Maier thought it was undemocratic to force people to wear seat belts. He also believed that the seat belts themselves could cause injuries. Maier said a person wearing a seat belt could be trapped in an overturned vehicle. He also argued that drivers wearing seat belts feel overconfident, so they drive with less care. He claimed that Alberta's seat belt law violated his right to security of person under the Charter of Rights and Freedoms.

Albertans were educated about the use of seat belts over a 3-year period . Although the law made wearing seat belts mandatory, and the number of Albertans wearing seat belts increased, the debate continued.

People who favour seat belt laws say wearing seat belts saves lives and reduces injuries in traffic accidents. In Saskatchewan, Manitoba, and British Columbia, road deaths either decreased or remained the same once the seat belt law went into effect. Supporting statistics from Canada and the United States show that injuries dropped more than 38 percent after seat belt laws were passed.

WELCOME TO THE POLICE STATE OF ALBERTA!

A 1976 study by the U.S. Department of Transport said that a seat belt law would prevent three times as many deaths and eight times as many injuries as reducing the speed limit to 95 kilometres per hour. Supporters of the seat belt law believe people must be required to wear seat belts. Statistics show that without seat belt laws only about 15 percent of drivers wear seat belts. With seat belt laws, more than 66 percent wear seat belts.

Before the law was introduced, few Albertans wore seat belts. In 1986, Transport Canada statistics showed that less than 28 percent of Albertans wore seat belts. Over the 19 months following the law, Alberta's seat belt use rose to 82 percent, the highest in Canada at that time. However, some citizens still disagreed with a law that forced them to wear seat belts.

Maier chose an unusual form of active citizenship. He decided to get arrested and then make his point in court. On the day the law was enacted in July 1987, Maier drove around downtown Calgary with this seat belt hanging out of his truck door. On the first day, he received a warning from police. Three days later, he was given a ticket and a $25 fine.

At first, Maier's protest was successful. The judge agreed that although the risk was small there was a chance that a seat belt could injure a driver. Therefore, Maier was within his rights to refuse to wear a seat belt.

The Alberta government appealed the decision. This time, a higher court, the Alberta Court of Appeal, looked at the total benefit to society. The court said there was enough evidence to show that seat belts save lives. Provincial statistics showed that during the time Alberta had a seat belt law traffic injuries decreased by 5 percent, and deaths decreased by 9 percent. The judge overturned the lower court's decision.

Maier's battle against mandatory seat belt use cost him $12,000 of his own money on legal fees and court costs.

Municipal Governments

Canada covers a large area. Therefore, the Constitution allows provincial governments to establish smaller municipal governments, which have power over many local concerns. There are two basic systems of municipal governments—urban and rural. Urban governments manage the affairs of people residing in towns and cities, while rural governments do the same for those living outside these areas.

Urban governments are run by politicians who are usually known as the city council. The city council is composed of councillors and led by a mayor. Councillors represent different sections of the city called wards. During elections, people in each ward vote for their councillor.

Rural governments are organized slightly differently. Since rural people usually live on farms scattered across large areas of land, the provinces divide these areas into townships. Instead of city councils, there are township councils, led by a reeve, who functions like a mayor. Other members, called township councillors, help the reeve make decisions. They perform duties similar to those carried out by city councillors.

Municipal governments make decisions at a more local level than federal or provincial governments. They consider issues involving street parking regulations, traffic lights, snow and garbage removal, and road repairs. They also make decisions regarding the location of public parks, arenas, and libraries. Municipal governments create bylaws regulating the duties of firefighters, police officers, and local businesses.

Many municipalities have a committee system to put policies in place. The committees study problems

Although Toronto is considered the financial hub of Canada, Toronto's municipal government faces problems such as youth unemployment, traffic congestion, rent increases, and homelessness.

and issues and make recommendations to the council. Frequently, the business of running the municipality is handled by one person, sometimes called the city manager. This person reports to council on the operation of the various departments. In small towns, a town administrator usually handles all of the town's affairs. The town administrator is responsible to the council.

Many municipal governments have groups that administer services such as the police force, parks, libraries, and local transportation. These groups operate independently, set their own policies, and review the operation of these services.

One of the most important responsibilities of municipal governments is education. Municipal governments form school boards to make decisions about education. People in the area vote for members of the school board called trustees. The board makes decisions about schools, books, buses, and teachers' salaries. It also decides how much people should pay to provide these services, and forwards this decision to the municipal government.

A municipal government can assess property taxes based on the value of the homes in its area. This level of government also receives money from the province in the form of grants.

One of the most difficult tasks for municipal governments is trying to provide the level of services that people want, while maintaining a balanced budget. The rising cost of equipment, buildings, and supplies, as well as the salary and wage needs of municipal employees makes the budget process a tough balancing act. At this level, the political process can be very

heated because so many decisions have immediate effects upon people's standard of living.

Many municipal governments have been forced to cut back their services to help provincial governments achieve balanced budgets. Cutbacks have created conflict between the provincial and municipal governments. Disagreements have occurred over the amount of provincial interference in municipal affairs because there is an overlap of power between these two levels of government.

If citizens are unhappy with the level of services, or if they want their council to address a specific issue, they have a chance to speak at regular council meetings. Usually, a certain amount of time is set aside for listening to citizens' concerns. Most often, the concerns are discussed and then directed to the proper officials for more study. Typically, citizens' concerns include road repairs and land-use issues.

Municipalities can sometimes get funding for infrastructure projects, such as roads and water treatment systems, from the federal government.

Executive Branch of Government

The executive branch of government makes decisions that affect Canadians' lives in many ways.

To make the governing of Canada an easier task, the federal government has three branches: executive, legislative, and judicial. Each branch is responsible for different tasks, and each operates as a check on the others' power. This system ensures that no single branch of government can become too powerful.

The executive branch of government makes decisions that affect Canadians' lives in many ways. This branch is made up of the prime minister and the cabinet.

The prime minister is the leader of the country. This position has both political and administrative functions. As leader of the party with the most seats in the House of Commons, the prime minister heads the cabinet and appoints its members. The prime minister and cabinet direct the intent and effect of government policies.

The leader of the official opposition balances the power of the prime minister in the House of Commons. The leader of the official opposition heads the party that received the second-highest number of seats in the House of Commons. This party receives special status as a kind of alternate government. They appoint a group of opposition members who act as watchdogs for cabinet posts. The opposition ensures that the governing party is responsible to the electorate.

Usually about thirty members of Parliament are appointed to the cabinet to serve as advisors to the prime minister. The prime minister generally tries to appoint cabinet ministers from each province to ensure that concerns from every area of the country are represented. If the government does not have

In 2004, Conservative Stephen Harper became leader of the official opposition. Harper's job was to ensure that the Liberal Party remained accountable to the public.

adequate representation in every province, the prime minister can appoint members of the Senate to the cabinet.

Most cabinet ministers have portfolios, which means they are in charge of government departments such as finance, external affairs, or the environment. Some ministers do not have portfolios. Ministers of state may be in charge of a specific section of a department within a ministry, such as the Ministry of State for Science and Technology. Cabinet ministers are accountable to the House of Commons for the actions of their departments and can be asked to resign if serious problems develop.

Cabinet ministers must support the decisions and policies of the cabinet, regardless of their personal beliefs. This means that even if a cabinet minister is very opposed to the decision ultimately made by cabinet, he or she must never admit this opposition once the cabinet decision is made public. Cabinet ministers who do not support the decisions of cabinet may be forced to resign their positions.

The cabinet is responsible for introducing most new legislation. It has the sole power to prepare and introduce new tax legislation and new laws regarding the spending of public money.

Prime Minister Paul Martin appointed a 38-member cabinet in July 2004.

Legislative Branch of Government

The second branch of government is closely connected to the first. The executive branch is a small part of the legislative branch. The legislative branch debates the need for proposed laws and votes on these laws. This branch consists of an elected assembly called the House of Commons and an appointed body known as the senate. The legislative branch of government passes laws regulating the conduct of Canadians.

The senate consists of 105 members, including twenty-four from the Maritime provinces (ten from Nova Scotia, ten from New Brunswick, and four from Prince Edward Island); six from Newfoundland and Labrador; twenty-four from Québec; twenty-four from Ontario; twenty-four from the Western Provinces (six from Manitoba, six from British Columbia, six from Saskatchewan, and six from Alberta); and one each from the Yukon Territory, the Northwest Territories, and Nunavut. There is also provision for four or eight extra senators—one or two from the Maritimes, Québec, Ontario, and the West.

The House of Commons is the most important lawmaking body in Canada and is made up of members of Parliament. Members of Parliament

Canada's Senators

Senators must...

- be appointed by the governor general on the advice of the Prime Minister
- be at least thirty years old
- have real estate worth $4,000, and total net assets worth at least $4,000.
- reside in the province or territory for which he or she is appointed.
- if chosen from Québec, he or she must reside in that province or own property in the senatorial district for which he or she is named.
- remain in office until age 75 (unless he or she misses two consecutive sessions in Parliament).

The Senate can...

- introduce any bills except those involving money.
- amend or reject any bill. It can even reject a bill as many times as it likes. A bill cannot become law until it has been passed in the Senate.
- form committees to listen to statements from groups and individuals who would be affected if a bill became law.

Riding Map

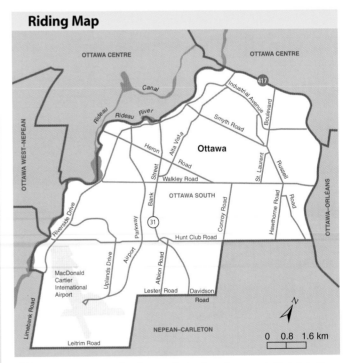

Elections Canada determines the electoral districts for federal elections. The Chief Electoral Officer for Canada determines the number of seats for each province and territory based on population and legislation.

represent the people in their ridings. In 2004, Canada was divided into 308 ridings, or constituencies. Each riding contains about the same number of people. The House of Commons is representative of Canada according to the population density of the country.

Most MPs belong to a political party, such as the Liberal Party, the Conservative Party, or the Bloc Québécois. Very few MPs run as independents, which means they represent their constituents without belonging to a political party.

When a political party wins a clear majority in the House of Commons, the cabinet from the old government resigns, and the governor general calls on the leader of the majority party to form the government. The prime minister chooses the cabinet ministers, and the governor general formally appoints them to their posts.

If no party receives a clear majority, the cabinet that was in office before and during the election has two choices. The cabinet ministers can resign, in which case the governor general will call on the leader of the largest opposition party to form a cabinet, or the cabinet already in office can choose to stay in office and try to lead the government with a minority government (one whose party has less than half the seats). In either case, MPs in the newly-elected Commons decide whether a minority government will stay in office or be replaced.

If a government loses a vote of non-confidence in the House of Commons, it must either resign or ask the governor general to dissolve Parliament and call an election. If the government resigns, then the official opposition becomes the government.

In rare circumstances, the governor general can refuse to call a new election. For example, if no party had a clear majority, and the prime minister asked for a new election without allowing the new Parliament to meet, the governor general would probably refuse. A newly-elected Parliament must meet and see if it can successfully conduct business. As well, if a minority government is defeated early in a Parliamentary session, and it appears possible that a government from another party can obtain the support of the House, then the governor general could refuse the request for a new election.

The legislative branch acts as a check on the powers of the cabinet. While the cabinet can lead, the senate and Commons can refuse to follow.

The House of Commons makes decisions by engaging in debate. Debates can become heated when the issue is controversial.

Legislative Process

Passing bills is one of the most important tasks of the legislative branch of government. A bill is a draft of a proposed law. Federal and provincial governments pass bills in a similar manner. Cabinet introduces proposed laws. These proposed laws are studied, debated, altered, and voted on before becoming law. The biggest difference is that provincial laws must be passed only once, while federal laws must be passed in both the House of Commons and the senate.

Two types of legislation can be introduced into Parliament: private and public bills. Private bills affect a single person or company and are fairly uncommon. Most private bills are introduced in the Senate and are passed quickly by the House of Commons.

Public bills concern public policy and affect all Canadians or a particular group of Canadians. A cabinet minister usually introduces public bills into the House of Commons. These are usually called government bills. All parties in the House of Commons usually debate public bills at length.

Public bills can also be introduced as a private members' bill, which means it is the bill of a single MP and does not originate with the government in power.

The governor general's signature is an important symbol of government power. It is required to make bills into law.

These bills are commonly used to pressure the government into taking some kind of action.

For a bill to pass, it must pass through several stages called "readings." This term refers to a time in parliamentary history when MPs had to actually read their bills out loud.

Once a bill has passed in the House of Commons, it goes to the senate where it undergoes a similar process. If the senate makes any changes, the House of Commons must review them. The House of Commons can amend the changes and send it back to the senate if it chooses. After passing in both houses, bills must be signed by the governor general, which is called receiving royal assent, to have the force of law.

The speaker of House of Commons is responsible for ensuring that the legislative process follows proper procedure.

IN-DEPTH

How a Bill is Passed

Every bill is read three times in each house. The first step is for the government to give members 2-days written notice that the bill will be announced.

The First Reading
- The bill's title is announced, usually by the minister responsible for it.
- The bill is usually automatically accepted and sent to be printed and distributed.
- There is no debate at this stage.

The Second Reading
- Usually occurs a few weeks later.
- The minister responsible for the bill will give a speech explaining the reasons for the new law.
- Members will debate the main purposes of the bill.
- The bill is sent to a committee for study. The committee can make amendments as it sees fit.
- The committee's work is sent back to the House in the report stage.

The Third Reading
- The House reviews the committee's recommendations and makes any amendments it chooses to adopt.
- Members have another chance to debate the bill.
- The House votes on the bill and then refers it to the senate where it undergoes a similar process.

Royal Assent
- Once the bill has passed in both houses, the governor general gives royal assent in a special ceremony in the Senate chambers.

The Judicial System

The last branch of Canadian government is the judicial branch. Canada has many levels in its court system. Each level administers a different part of the law. This system was established by the Constitution Act, 1867 (formerly called the British North America Act, 1867), which gave the federal government control over criminal law and procedure. Provinces were given control of the administration of justice in their province.

The highest court in Canada is called the Supreme Court. This court, which meets in Ottawa, is the final place for appeals. It consists of nine judges, including the chief justice. The Supreme Court must interpret laws regarding Canada's Constitution. Many cases have been heard by the Supreme Court, and their decisions have had an impact on all Canadians. For instance, a 1975 Supreme Court decision forced the provinces to enact matrimonial property laws that recognize a spouse's contribution, whether financial or otherwise, to family assets. This meant that divorcing couples now had to consider the contributions of non-working spouses as part of the family assets.

The Supreme Court's rulings play a role in the decisions made by other courts. Sometimes the Supreme Court refuses to rule on a controversial matter if it feels the legislation is unclear. The government is then asked to create new legislation. This process acts as a check on the power of the legislative and executive branches by ensuring that Canadians have control over their laws.

The Federal Court of Canada is under the Supreme Court. It deals mainly with federal taxation laws,

The Supreme Court of Canada

The Supreme Court was created by the Constitution Act, 1867. The first laws necessary to create a Supreme Court were introduced in the Parliament of Canada in 1869 and 1870 and then withdrawn. On April 8, 1875, however, a law was passed that created the Supreme Court of Canada.

In the early days, the Supreme Court was not the court of last resort for cases in Canada. All cases could be appealed to the Judicial Committee of the Privy Council in London, England. As well, cases could by-pass the Court and go directly to London from the provincial courts of appeal. The Supreme Court became the court of last resort for criminal appeals in 1933. It became the court of last resort for all other cases in 1949.

Under Canadian law, the governor general appoints all justices of the Supreme Court. However, it is traditional for the prime minister to control who is appointed. Québécois, by law, must hold three of the nine positions on the Supreme Court of Canada.

In practice, the remaining six positions are divided in the following manner: three from Ontario, two from the western provinces and one from the Atlantic provinces.

The prime minister's choice of chief justice does not require approval and is not subject to review. A Supreme Court justice serves until he or she retires or, at latest, is 75 years old.

■ It is customary to address a Supreme Court Judge as "Justice."

copyrights, claims against the federal government, and claims arising from federal statutes.

The minister of justice appoints most federal judges. Sometimes the prime minister appoints them. To become a federal judge, candidates must be lawyers who have been members of a provincial bar association for 10 years. Judges are most often chosen from a lower court. After their appointment, judges can only be removed by a decision from both the House of Commons and the senate. The Canadian Judicial Council reviews complaints against judges and, when necessary, recommends appropriate disciplinary measures to the minister of justice.

Provincial Courts

Provincial courts handle provincial or municipal cases and less severe criminal cases, such as theft. They decide when there is enough evidence for more serious crimes, such as murder, to go to trial. Provinces and territories also have higher courts that hear serious criminal cases and all civil cases, such as divorce and injury claims. The three senior courts are the County Court, which is a trial court with limited civil and criminal jurisdiction; the Supreme Court, which is a trial court with unlimited civil and criminal jurisdiction; and the Court of Appeal, which reviews the decisions of lower courts when asked to do so. The appeal court does not hear new evidence but considers the facts in the original case.

The attorney general of each province usually appoints provincial judges. In some provinces, the attorney general only appoints a judge after a special committee reviews the candidate. Unlike federal judges, provincial judges can be appointed after serving at the bar for 5 years. Once appointed, judges can only be removed through an impeachment process in which a provincial judicial council investigates the allegations against a judge, makes a review, and provides recommendations on discipline. Provincial judges usually hold office until age 70.

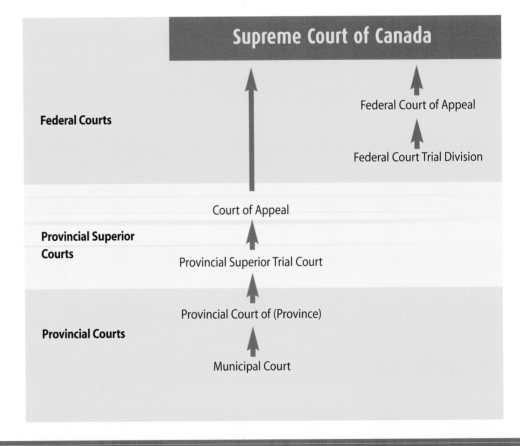

The Nunavut Court of Justice

The Nunavut Court of Justice is Canada's first, and only, single-level court. It came into existence in Nunavut on April 1, 1999. This court system evolved over several years through a consultative process that required federal and territorial legislative amendments.

Before April 1, 1999, the area now known as Nunavut had a territorial court and the Northwest Territories (NWT) Supreme Court. The Supreme Court was the highest court and had more power or jurisdiction than the territorial court. Now, in Nunavut, there is just one court. This court combines the jurisdiction or power of the two NWT courts under one judicial roof. In a large territory such as Nunavut, it seemed sensible for one court to handle all cases.

The Nunavut Court of Justice covers the entire territory of Nunavut and travels to approximately 85 percent of the communities across the territory. The Court does not travel to smaller communities that report very little crime. These communities usually have no police presence.

The Court travels to different communities every 6 weeks to 2 years, depending on the number of cases in a community. On average, the Nunavut Court of Justice has 2 to 3 court sittings per week each year. Each week, there is at least one travelling court circuit and one court sitting in Iqaluit.

The circuit court is comprised of a judge, clerk, court reporter, prosecutor, and at least one defence attorney. Interpreters are often hired in the community, but at times, they travel with the circuit court.

Nunavut plans to replace its old courthouse with a new Justice Centre in 2006.

Court can be held in community halls, school gyms, and other conference facilities. All court proceedings are interpreted for the public. Elders and justices of the peace sit with the judge in the courtroom. They are allowed to speak with the accused after he or she has been found guilty and before a sentence is passed.

Checks and Balances

A House of Commons committee is a group of people assembled to research certain bills, act as liaisons between the public and the government, and make suggestions to the House of Commons.

Canada's three branches of government act as a system of checks and balances for each other. No one branch can abuse its power as the other two have the ability to check its activities. In this way, power is kept in balance between the three branches.

The most important check on government power is active citizen participation. By participating, citizens can ensure their government is democratic, responsible, and representative. The most basic way to participate is, of course, through elections. The main purpose of an election is to pick the candidates that best represent citizens' interests.

Citizens can also influence the decision-making process of the nation by participating in the committees of the senate and the House of Commons. After a bill has been debated in second reading, it is sent to a Commons committee, which often meets with interested citizens or groups to hear their views on the bill. To further assist in government decision making, Canadians can share their views on certain matters in commissions of inquiry, which try to determine the facts of a specific event or policy issue, and task forces, which are legislative committees authorized by legislative leaders to study a specific subject for a certain period of time.

At times, an issue is so important that the government wants to know how the majority of the country feels about it. During these times, a government can hold a plebiscite or referendum.

National Referendums

In Canada's history, there have been only three national referendums. The first referendum was held in 1898. It asked voters to decide whether the sale and use of alcohol should be prohibited. Even though the majority of people voted in favour of a law prohibiting the sale and use of alcohol, the majority was so small that the government did not pass the law.

The second referendum was held in 1942. It was on the question of conscription. The government wanted to find out if citizens agreed with its proposal that people be legally required to join the armed forces. The law was intended to get more Québec citizens into the services. Although Canada's citizens voted 80 percent in favour of conscription, the people of Québec voted about 70 percent against it. A conscription law was enacted before the end of the war.

The third national referendum was held in 1992 to consider the Charlottetown Accord for a renewed federal structure. More than 54 percent of Canadians voted against the referendum. As a result of this referendum, the Charlottetown Accord did not become law.

The 1942 referendum on conscription strained French and English relations in Canada.

A plebiscite is a vote designed to measure public opinion on an issue. Anyone who can vote in a general election can vote in a plebiscite. Governments are not bound to follow the results of the plebiscite, although elected officials would normally not ignore such a decision from their constituents.

A referendum is similar to a plebiscite, except the results are binding. Governments usually follow the results of a referendum when formulating their policy decisions. Provinces and municipalities can also hold referendums. In most cases, these referendums are held when a minimum number of eligible voters signs a petition calling for a referendum.

Canada's system of checks and balances, as well as the many opportunities it gives its citizens to participate, helps prevent the abuse of power by individuals or organizations. This ensures that democracy guides Canadian government decisions.

Time Line

1500s The Mohawks, Oneidas, Onondagas, Cayugas, and Seneca form the the League of the Iroquois.

1774 The Québec Act guarantees religious freedom for Roman Catholic colonists.

1791 The Constitutional Act, 1791 grants representative government with limited powers for elected representatives. The act divides Québec into Upper and Lower Canada.

1835 Joseph Howe, editor of the *NovaScotian* newspaper, calls for responsible government in Nova Scotia.

1848 Responsible government is granted in Nova Scotia and New Brunswick "without a blow struck or pane of glass broken."

1849 Responsible government is established in Nova Scotia and the Province of Canada.

1851 Prince Edward Island achieves responsible government.

1855 Newfoundland is granted responsible government.

1857 Queen Victoria names Ottawa as Canada's capital.

1867 Nova Scotia, New Brunswick, Québec, and Ontario form a confederation called the Dominion of Canada.

1867 The Constitution Act, 1867 creates the Supreme Court of Canada.

1898 The first national referendum is held on the question of prohibiting the sale and use of alcohol.

1931 The Statute of Westminster grants Canada independence from Great Britain. However, changes to the Canadian Constitution still need to be approved by the British Parliament.

1942 The second national referendum is held on the question of conscription.

1944 Saskatchewan voters elect the first socialist government in North America, led by Tommy Douglas.

1949 The Supreme Court becomes the court of last resort for all cases.

1952 Vincent Massey is the first Canadian appointed governor general.

1969 The federal government becomes officially bilingual.

1975 A Supreme Court decision results in a change in the matrimonial property laws to recognize a spouse's contribution to family assets.

1980 The majority of Québécois reject separation from Canada in a referendum vote.

1982 The new Canadian Constitution is ratified by every province except Québec.

1992 The third national referendum is held. It asks voters to approve the Charlottetown Accord for a renewed federal structure.

1993 Kim Campbell becomes first female prime minister.

1995 The Québec referendum rejects separation from Canada by a small majority.

1999 The new territory of Nunavut is formed. It is the first territory in Canada to have a majority indigenous population.

Quiz (answers on page 47)

Multiple Choice

Choose the best answer in the multiple choice questions that follow.

1 Canadian government is based on what principle?

a) dictatorship
b) representative democracy
c) monarchy
d) oligarchy

2 Which Aboriginal group practised democracy before Europeans arrived in North America?

a) Inuit
b) Cree
c) Iroquois
d) Hopi

3 Where was Tommy Douglas born?

a) Ontario
b) Scotland
c) Manitoba
d) Saskatchewan

4 Before responsible government in Canada, decisions were made by what type of government?

a) aristocracy
b) dictatorship
c) democracy
d) oligarchy

5 Who represents the Queen in Canada?

a) governor general
b) prime minister
c) member of Parliament
d) chief justice of the Supreme Court

6 Statistics Canada is a government agency responsible for what job?

a) maintaining highways
b) collecting taxes
c) collecting statistics such as employment or inflation rates
d) ensuring the security of Canada

Mix and Match

Match the description in column A with the correct term in column B. There are more terms than descriptions.

A	B
1. Seat belt use rose to 82 percent in this province.	a) Northwest Territories
2. Education is an important responsibility for this level of government.	b) prime minister
3. This person is the elected leader of Canada.	c) Nunavut
4. Most MPs belong to this type of group.	d) Alberta
5. A bill passes through three of these stages before it becomes law.	e) readings
6. This territory has a one-level court.	f) Queen of Canada
	g) Nova Scotia
	h) political party
	i) municipal

Time Line

Find the appropriate spot on the time line for each event listed below.

A Saskatchewan voters elect the first socialist government in North America.

B The first national referendum in Canada.

C Joseph Howe publishes a letter exposing the dishonesty of several Halifax judges.

D The new Canadian Constitution is ratified by every province except Québec.

E The League of the Iroquois is formed.

F Nunavut is created.

1300 1

1774 Québec Act guarantees religious freedom for Roman Catholic colonists.

1791 The Constitutional Act divides Québec into Upper and Lower Canada.

1835 2

1841 The Act of Union unites Upper and Lower Canada.

1848 Responsible government is established in Nova Scotia and the Province of Canada

1857 Queen Victoria names Ottawa as Canada's capital.

1867 Nova Scotia, New Brunswick, Québec and Ontario form the Dominion of Canada.

1867 Sir John A. Macdonald becomes Canada's first prime minister.

1898 3

1926 Old age pension instituted by the federal government.

1944 4

1969 The federal government becomes officially bilingual.

1980 The majority of Québécois reject separatism.

1982 5

1993 Kim Campbell becomes Canada's first female prime minister.

1995 The Québec referendum narrowly rejects separation from Canada.

1999 6

Further Research

Suggested Reading

Nicol, Eric. *Canadian Politics Unplugged.* Toronto: Dundurn Press, 2003.

Quinlan, Don, Mary Jane Pickup, and Terry Lahey. *Government: Participating in Canada.* Toronto: Oxford University Press, 1999.

Tammemagi, Hans. *Exploring the Hill: An Intimate Look at Canada's Parliament.* Toronto: Fitzhenry & Whiteside, 2002.

Tindal, C. Richard. *A Citizen's Guide to Government.* Toronto: McGraw-Hill Ryerson, 2000.

Internet Resources

Canada: A People's History Online
history.cbc.ca
The online companion to CBC's award-winning television series on the history of Canada, as told through the eyes of its people. This multimedia Web site features behind-the-scenes information, games, puzzles, and discussion boards. The site is also available in French.

The Canadian Encyclopedia Online
www.thecanadianencyclopedia.com
A reference for all things Canadian. In-depth history articles are accompanied by photographs, paintings, and maps. All articles can be read in both French and English.

Some Web sites stay current longer than others. To find other Web sites that deal with Canada's system of government, enter terms such as "House of Commons," "Senate," and "Supreme Court" into a search engine.

Glossary

benevolence: an act intending or showing kindness and good will

bills: proposed laws brought before a provincial legislature or Parliament for reading, debate, study, and possible approval

cabinet: a group of members of Parliament chosen by the prime minister to head government departments and develop policies and plans to govern the country

censure: harsh criticism or disapproval

citizenship: a process in which citizens participate in Canadian life at the individual, community, and societal level

impartially: to treat all equally

interest group: a group of people sharing common concerns and trying to influence governments at different levels

jurisdiction: the area within which power can be exercised

justice: just, fair, and right treatment

monarchs: people who reign over kingdoms or empires

Parliament: the central government; composed of the House of Commons, the senate, and the monarchy

political party: a group of people who share similar ideas about how government should operate

power: the ability to act, control, or influence

probate: establish the legal validity of wills and other documents

public hearing: a meeting at which individual citizens and groups give their opinions about problems being studied

rights: privileges protected by law and agreed to belong to all citizens based on common beliefs about justice

Answers

Multiple Choice	Mix and Match	Time Line
1. b)	1. d)	1. e)
2. c)	2. i)	2. c)
3. b)	3. b)	3. b)
4. d)	4. h)	4. a)
5. a)	5. e)	5. d)
6. c)	6. c)	6. f)

Index